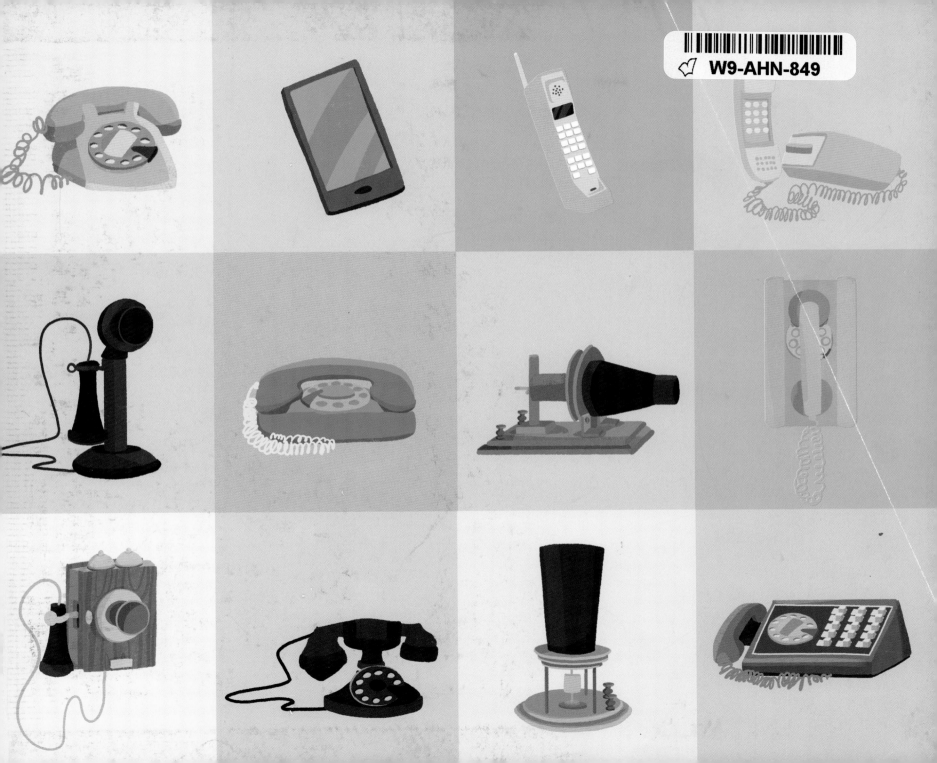

PHONES
KEEP US CONNECTED

BY KATHLEEN WEIDNER ZOEHFELD · ILLUSTRATED BY KASIA NOWOWIEJSKA

HARPER
An Imprint of HarperCollinsPublishers

Special thanks to Dr. Jerry Gibson, Distinguished Professor, Department of Electrical and Computer Engineering at the University of California, Santa Barbara, for his valuable assistance.

The Let's-Read-and-Find-Out Science book series was originated by Dr. Franklyn M. Branley, Astronomer Emeritus and former Chairman of the American Museum of Natural History–Hayden Planetarium, and was formerly co-edited by him and Dr. Roma Gans, Professor Emeritus of Childhood Education, Teachers College, Columbia University. Text and illustrations for each of the books in the series are checked for accuracy by an expert in the relevant field. For more information about Let's-Read-and-Find-Out Science books, write to HarperCollins Children's Books, 195 Broadway, New York, NY 10007, or visit our website at www.letsreadandfindout.com.

Let's Read-and-Find-Out Science® is a trademark of HarperCollins Publishers.

ISBN 978-0-06-238668-7 (trade bdg.) — ISBN 978-0-06-238667-0 (pbk.)

The artist used Adobe Photoshop CC to create the digital illustrations for this book.
Typography by Erica De Chavez
16 17 18 19 20 SCP 10 9 8 7 6 5 4 3 2 1 ❖ First Edition

For Beth, Connie, Martha,
Nina, Sue, and Wendy—may
we always stay connected.
—K.Z.

For Filip, Marta, and Piotr,
my great friends
—K.N.

You asked your friend to meet you at the soccer game.
There she is—WAY across on the other side of the field.
"Over here!" you shout.
But your friend doesn't hear you. You're too far away.

No problem. Just grab your phone
and give her a call.
You and your friend are connected!

It doesn't matter how far away your friend is. You can always say hello!
But it wasn't always that way. Before phones were invented, if you
wanted to wish your friend a happy birthday, you could mail her a card. But
there was no way she could hear your voice, unless you went to visit her.

LETTER BOX

Whenever you speak, you make the vocal cords in your throat vibrate. Those vibrations set the air around them vibrating, too. The vibrations move through the air in waves, called sound waves.

A loud sound has a lot of energy. But no matter how loud a sound is to begin with, the waves can only go so far before they begin to run out of energy and fade. People tried all kinds of ways to send their voices farther.

Did You Know?

Sound waves need something to travel through—such as air or water or even a solid object. If you clap your hands in outer space, a person right next to you wouldn't be able to hear it, since the sound would have nothing to travel through.

In the early 1800s, a few scientists discovered that sound could be sent along a straight wire. The solid wire helped the sound waves travel better than they do through air. You can do an experiment yourself, to find out how this works.

Make a String Telephone

You'll need:
- Measuring tape
- A ball of string
- Scissors
- Two paper cups
- A large needle

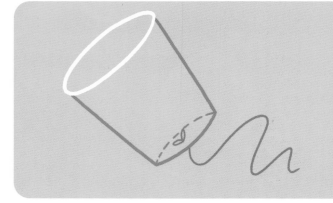

- Measure and cut a piece of string about 10 feet (3 meters) long.
- Use the needle to poke a small hole in the center of the bottom of each cup.
- Thread one end of the string through the bottom of one cup and make a small knot in the string to keep it from pulling out.
- Then do the same with the other cup.

Have your friend hold one cup, and you hold the other. Stretch the string out between you, gently, until it is straight and tight.

Have your friend hold her cup up to her ear while you quietly say something into your cup. Then say the same words to her, without the string phone. Which way did your friend hear you better?

When you speak into the cup, the sound of your voice makes the air in the cup vibrate. And that makes the bottom of the cup vibrate. The vibrations move quickly through the string. That makes the bottom of the other cup vibrate in the same way as the bottom of your cup. Those vibrations become sound waves that travel through the air in your friend's cup. And she hears your voice, as if you were right up close.

A wire or string phone might help people talk to each other in the same house. But it didn't solve the big problem: how to make the sound of your voice travel FAR!

In the 1830s, inventors figured out how to use the energy of electricity to send coded messages. The new invention was called the electrical telegraph. Samuel Morse created a simple code of dots and dashes.

Happy Birthday

MORSE CODE CHART

A	•-	N	-•	O	-----
B	-•••	O	---	1	•----
C	-•-•	P	•--•	2	••---
D	-••	Q	--•-	3	•••--
E	•	R	•-•	4	••••-
F	••-•	S	•••	5	•••••
G	--•	T	-	6	-••••
H	••••	U	••-	7	--•••
I	••	V	•••-	8	----••
J	•---	W	•--	9	----•
K	-•-	X	-••-	.	•-•-•-
L	•-••	Y	-•--	;	--•-•-
M	--	Z	--••	?	••--••

Wires were strung up all around the world. People were amazed
by how fast and how far electricity could carry their messages.

It wasn't long before some people, such as Alexander Graham Bell,
started wondering: Could electricity be used to carry the human voice
over long distances, too?

15

Bell was a speech teacher. He spent most of his time helping deaf children learn to talk. What Bell wanted more than anything was for people to be able to speak to and understand each other. He didn't know a lot about electricity. But he studied and learned as much about it as he could.

In 1876, he and his assistant, Thomas Watson, were working on improving the telegraph when they made an interesting discovery. One of the metal springs on Watson's telegraph got stuck to its magnet. He plucked it loose.

"Twang!" went the spring.

Over in the next room, Bell's telegraph was connected to Watson's. And Bell heard the spring on his telegraph twang, too!

"What did you do?" shouted Bell.

"I plucked the spring," said Watson.

"Do it again!" cried Bell.

Watson did. Again, the spring in Bell's telegraph made the same twanging sound.

From that point on, Bell knew that an electrical current could carry a complex sound. If it could do that, maybe it really could carry the human voice!

Bell and Watson were finally ready to build their first phone. Here's how it worked:

TRANSMITTER:
This is the part that sends, or transmits, your voice.

Mouthpiece:
You speak into the opening of the mouthpiece.

Diaphragm:
A very thin sheet of metal that vibrates easily—like the bottom of the paper cup in your string telephone experiment!

Wire:
The wire carries the electrical signal to the receiver.

Magnet:
A magnet is attached to the diaphragm. When the diaphragm vibrates, it makes the magnet vibrate. The vibrating magnet causes a wavy, vibrating flow of electricity.

18

RECEIVER:
This is the part that gets, or receives, your voice.

Earpiece:
You put your ear against the opening in the earpiece.

Diaphragm:
The diaphragm turns the electrical signal back into sound waves.

Wire:
The electrical waves made by the magnet pulse through the wire in a pattern. The pattern is exactly like the pattern of sound waves made by your voice.

Bell and Watson kept experimenting. They soon knew there were two ways to change sound into electricity. One was to use a moving magnet to create the vibrating flow of electricity. That's how they made their first phone. But they weren't very happy with its sound.

Battery-powered transmitter

Acid cup

Receiver

Thomas Edison worked on the problem. He made a small packet filled with little grains of carbon that could be used instead of the acid. Of all the inventions for making phones easy to build and use, Edison's worked best.

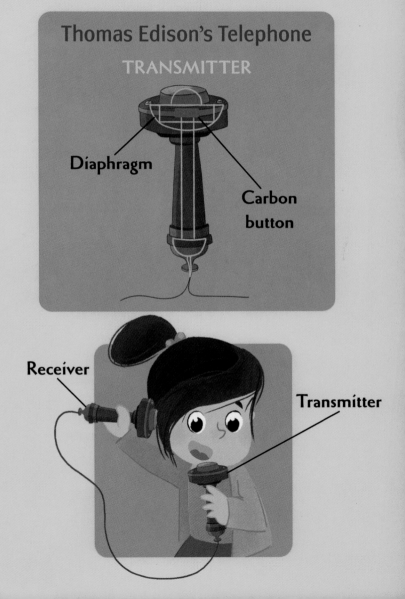

Thomas Edison's Telephone

TRANSMITTER

Diaphragm

Carbon button

Receiver

Transmitter

So they tried the second way. They used a battery to create a steady flow of electricity through the wires. They set up the transmitter so that the vibrations of the diaphragm would make the strength of that electrical flow vary. The varying strength of the electrical flow would match the pattern of sound waves made by your voice. This new phone's sound was much clearer.

From the start, the battery-powered phone worked better than the moving-magnet phone. But Bell's phone needed a small, open cup of acid in order to work. Building and using it was not easy—or safe!

Wires had already been strung up everywhere for telegraphs. Telegraph poles were quickly put to use to string up wires for the new telephones.

For the first time, people far away from one another could have conversations. We were connected!

Even today, the transmitters and receivers in phones work very much like they did in the time of Bell and Edison. But those phones needed wires.

You can call up your friend when she's on the other side of the soccer field. Or anywhere else you can think of! How do you send your voice across many miles, without any wires?

Instead of wires, your cell phone uses a form of energy called radio waves.

Not long after the first telephones were invented, Heinrich Hertz and others began experimenting with radio waves.

To send a radio broadcast, you need an antenna. That's a device that can create radio waves by generating back-and-forth bursts of electricity. Then you need a microphone. This is like a telephone's transmitter. It turns the sound waves into an electrical signal. That signal makes small changes in the radio waves—in a pattern exactly matching the vibrations of your voice. The radio waves carry the signal out.

Lots of people can listen to your radio broadcast. Your friend is one of your biggest fans, so he has his radio tuned to pick up your show's radio waves. His radio's receiver—like the telephone's receiver—turns them back into an electrical signal. And his radio's built-in speaker—like the phone's diaphragm—turns the signal into the sound of your voice.

Radio Waves

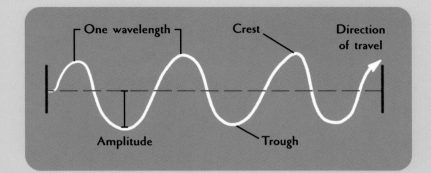

- One wavelength
- Crest
- Direction of travel
- Amplitude
- Trough

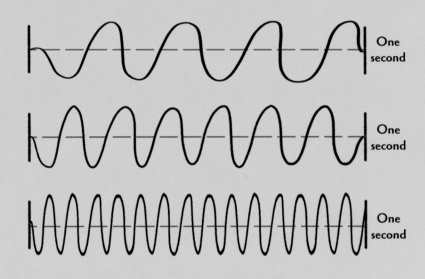

One second

One second

One second

Waves have ups and downs—called crests and troughs. The distance between two crests is the wavelength. The number of ups and downs that occur each second is the frequency of the wave. Each radio station's antenna sends out its waves at a particular frequency. You can tune your radio to pick up the frequency of your favorite station.

Your cell phone is like a tiny radio station. It has a small built-in antenna. It can send out radio waves. And it can receive them, too.

A battery gives your phone its power. The phone uses this power to create radio waves. But how can your little phone connect to a phone that is thousands of miles away? It doesn't have to. It only has to send to or receive from the nearest cellular antenna.

That antenna can send your signal out to a switching center, where it travels through wires or optical fiber to a switching center closer to your friend. From there it is sent to the cellular antenna nearest to your friend's phone.

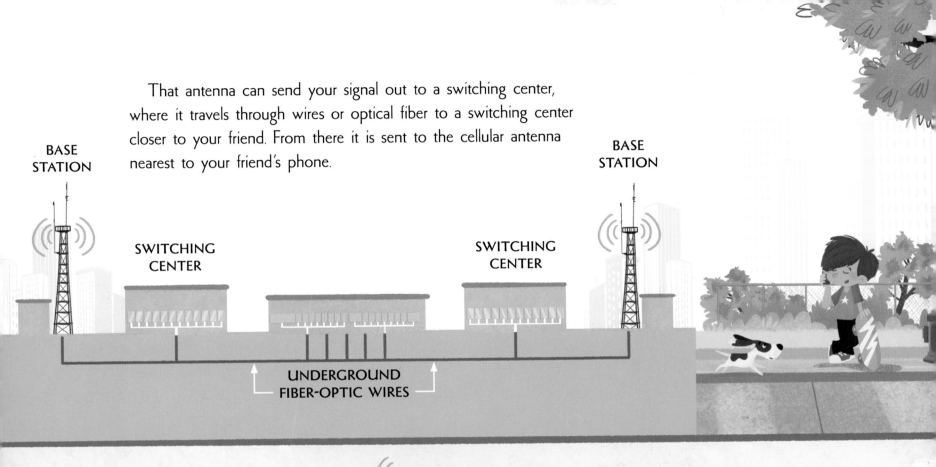

BASE STATION

BASE STATION

SWITCHING CENTER

SWITCHING CENTER

UNDERGROUND FIBER-OPTIC WIRES

Even when you call your friend at the soccer field, the radio waves carrying your voice do not go straight to your friend's phone. They first travel to the nearest cellular antenna and then to his phone.

27

Like the phones of Bell and Edison, your cell phone changes your voice into an electrical signal. But your cell phone has a new addition. It has a built-in computer. The computer changes that electrical signal into computer code.

INSIDE VIEW OF YOUR PHONE

Speaker (Receiver)

Antenna

Computer

Battery

Microphone (Transmitter)

010110010110101100100100110101101010101011001001011010101100100010101010110111

INSIDE VIEW OF YOUR PHONE

Back in the 1970s, the first wireless phones were as big as a brick and almost as heavy.

The pattern of the code makes small changes in the radio waves your phone sends out. The antenna nearest your friend picks up your code and sends it to his phone. The computer in his phone decodes it and turns it back into an electrical signal. And the receiver changes the signal into the sound of your voice.

Over the years, new inventions have made all the parts that make up your cell phone—from its battery and antenna to the electrical pathways on its computer chips—much smaller and lighter. That's why your phone is so small and yet can do so many things.

Alexander Graham Bell put together old discoveries about sound and electricity and he came up with a great new invention. A hundred years after Bell, inventors put together ideas about radio waves and the telephone and came up with another invention—the cell phone.

Scientists and inventors continue to put old discoveries together in new ways. But today we have many more discoveries and inventions to work with than Bell did!

What else do you wish your phone could do? Be sure to write down your ideas and draw sketches. That way you'll remember them. If you keep at it, you'll be able to develop your ideas over time and share them with others. Your new inventions will spring from the old inventions that have become a part of our everyday world.

Glossary

Antenna: A device used to send or receive radio, television, or cell phone signals. A sending antenna changes electrical energy into electromagnetic radiation. A receiving antenna does the opposite.

Carbon: A common element that is one of the building blocks of all living things. In nature, carbon can also be found in coal, in charcoal, and in graphite, which is used to make pencils.

Diaphragm: A very thin, usually disk-shaped object that vibrates easily when hit by sound waves.

Electricity: Electricity is a form of energy. It can be created by a battery or by a moving magnet or in a few other ways. Electricity can be made to flow through a wire. Electrical energy can be changed into other forms of energy.

Frequency: The number of up and down cycles per second of any wave motion.

Radio waves: Radio waves are one form of energy called electromagnetic radiation. Electromagnetic radiation is generated throughout the universe by the Sun and other stars. Light, heat, and X-rays are other types of electromagnetic radiation.

Receiver: A device that picks up, or receives, radio waves or electrical signals and turns them into sound waves.

Sound waves: Vibrations that move through air or through some other substance. All sound waves are created by a vibrating object of some kind.

Telegraph: Any device used to send messages across great distances. An electrical telegraph uses the energy of electricity to send its signals.

Transmitter: A device used to send out, or transmit, electrical signals or radio waves.

Vibrate: To move quickly, and continuously, back and forth or up and down. A vibrating object sets the air around it vibrating. And we hear the vibrations as sound.

FIND OUT MORE

Building a Better String Phone

Did you follow the instructions for building a string phone? How did it work? Do you wonder if you could make it work better? If so, then you have the mind of an inventor!

It's time to start experimenting! Make sure you have a notebook and pencil handy so you can keep track of your results.

Maybe you have some ideas for improving your phone already. If not, here are a few questions to get you started:

- Would my phone sound better if I used a different kind of string? You could try it out with yarn, fishing line, or thread.
- Would a longer string make the sound better or worse, or would the sound stay the same? Can I make my phone work with a *very* long string?
- Will my phone work if I bend the string around a corner? What about if someone holds on to the string in the center?
- The instructions said to stretch the string out until it is straight and tight. Why? What happens if you let the string hang loose? Is the sound better or worse or the same?

- Would my phone be easier to build if I used tape instead of small knots to hold the string on the bottoms of the cups? Will the tape make the sound better or worse, or will it stay the same?
- Maybe you'd like to make your phone look prettier. What will happen if I decorate the cups with paint or with construction paper and glue? Will the sound be better or worse or the same?

When you're done experimenting, draw a picture of your very own new and improved string phone in your notebook. Be sure to add labels and notes so you remember how you built it!

35

A Short History of the Phone

1876

The first telephone was invented by Alexander Graham Bell. "Mr. Watson—come here—I want to see you!" was the first sentence heard over the phone.

1900–1910

Telephones take off.

OF PHONES

Year	Phones (millions)
1900	0.6
1905	2.2
1910	5.8

(MILLIONS)

1919

Rotary dial phone was invented.

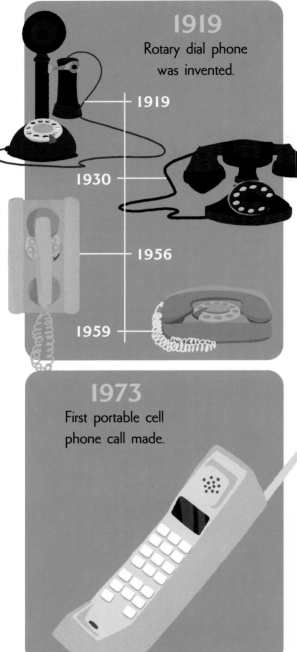

1919

1930

1956

1959

1927

The first two-way phone call that crossed an ocean was made..

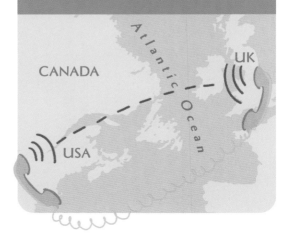

CANADA

Atlantic Ocean

UK

USA

1968

911 was chosen as the emergency number.

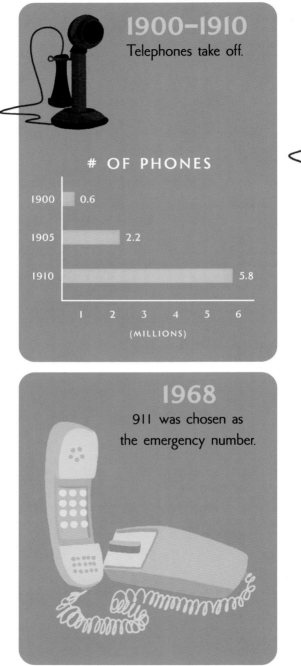

1973

First portable cell phone call made.

This book aligns with the Next Generation Science Standards.
Find out more at nextgenscience.org.

This book meets the Common Core State Standards for Science and
Technical Subjects. For Common Core resources for this title and others,
please visit www.readcommoncore.com.

Be sure to look for all of these books in the

Let's-Read-and-Find-Out Science series:

LEVEL 1

The Human Body:
How Many Teeth?
I'm Growing!
My Feet
My Five Senses
My Hands
Sleep Is for Everyone
What's For Lunch?

Plants and Animals:
Animals in Winter
Baby Whales Drink Milk
Big Tracks, Little Tracks
Bugs Are Insects
Dinosaurs Big and Small
Ducks Don't Get Wet
Fireflies in the Night
From Caterpillar to Butterfly
From Seed to Pumpkin
From Tadpole to Frog
How Animal Babies Stay Safe
How a Seed Grows
A Nest Full of Eggs
Starfish
A Tree Is a Plant
What Lives in a Shell?
What's Alive?
What's It Like to Be a Fish?
Where Are the Night Animals?
Where Do Chicks Come From?

The World Around Us:
Air Is All Around You
The Big Dipper
Clouds
Is There Life in Outer Space?
Pop!
Snow Is Falling
Sounds All Around
The Sun and the Moon
What Makes a Shadow?

LEVEL 2

The Human Body:
A Drop of Blood
Germs Make Me Sick!
Hear Your Heart
The Skeleton Inside You
What Happens to a Hamburger?
Why I Sneeze, Shiver, Hiccup, and Yawn
Your Skin and Mine

Plants and Animals:
Almost Gone
Ant Cities
Be a Friend to Trees
Chirping Crickets
Corn Is Maize
Dolphin Talk
Honey in a Hive
How Do Apples Grow?
How Do Birds Find Their Way?
Life in a Coral Reef
Look Out for Turtles!
Milk from Cow to Carton
An Octopus Is Amazing
Penguin Chick
Sharks Have Six Senses
Snakes Are Hunters
Spinning Spiders
Sponges Are Skeletons
What Color Is Camouflage?
Who Eats What?
Who Lives in an Alligator Hole?
Why Do Leaves Change Color?
Why Frogs Are Wet
Wiggling Worms at Work
Zipping, Zapping, Zooming Bats

Dinosaurs:
Did Dinosaurs Have Feathers?
Digging Up Dinosaurs
Dinosaur Bones
Dinosaur Tracks
Dinosaurs Are Different
Fossils Tell of Long Ago
My Visit to the Dinosaurs
What Happened to the Dinosaurs?
Where Did Dinosaurs Come From?

Space:
Floating in Space
The International Space Station
Mission to Mars
The Moon Seems to Change
The Planets in Our Solar System
The Sky Is Full of Stars
The Sun
What Makes Day and Night
What the Moon Is Like

Weather and the Seasons:
Down Comes the Rain
Feel the Wind
Flash, Crash, Rumble, and Roll
Hurricane Watch
Sunshine Makes the Seasons
Tornado Alert
What Will the Weather Be?

Our Earth:
Archaeologists Dig for Clues
Earthquakes
Flood Warning
Follow the Water from Brook to Ocean
How Deep Is the Ocean?
How Mountains Are Made
In the Rainforest
Let's Go Rock Collecting
Oil Spill!
Volcanoes
What Happens to Our Trash?
What's So Bad About Gasoline?
Where Do Polar Bears Live?
Why Are the Ice Caps Melting?
You're Aboard Spaceship Earth

The World Around Us:
Day Light, Night Light
Energy Makes Things Happen
Forces Make Things Move
Gravity Is a Mystery
How People Learned to Fly
Light Is All Around Us
Phones Keep Us Connected
Simple Machines
Switch On, Switch Off
What Is the World Made Of?
What Makes a Magnet?
Where Does the Garbage Go?